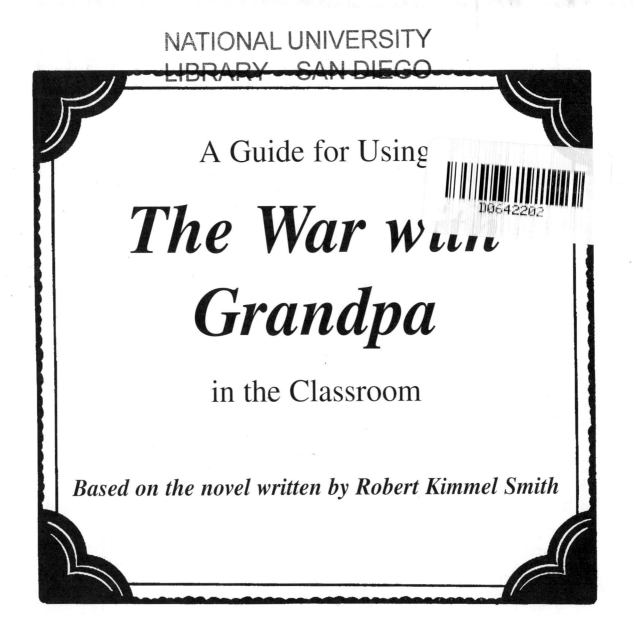

A Guide for Using

The War with Grandpa

in the Classroom

Based on the novel written by Robert Kimmel Smith

This guide written by **Karen Leiviska, M.S. Ed.**

Teacher Created Materials, Inc.
6421 Industry Way
Westminster, CA 92683
www.teachercreated.com
©1999 Teacher Created Materials
Reprinted, 2001
Made in U.S.A.
ISBN 1-57690-334-6

Edited by
Dona Herweck Rice

Illustrated by
Wendy Chang

Cover Art by
Dennis Carmichael

Table of Contents

Introduction

A good book can touch our lives like a good friend. It can stimulate our imaginations, inform our minds, inspire our higher selves, and fill our time with magic! With a good book, we are never lonely or bored. A good book only gets better with time because each reading brings us new meaning. Each new story is a treasure to cherish forever.

In Literature Units, we take great care to select books that will become treasured friends for life.

Teachers using this unit will find the following features to supplement their own valuable ideas.

- Sample Lesson Plan

- Pre-reading Activities

- A Biographical Sketch and Picture of the Author

- A Book Summary

- Vocabulary Lists and Suggested Vocabulary Activity Ideas

- Chapters grouped, with each section including the following:

    —*a quiz*

    —*a hands-on project*

    —*a cooperative learning activity*

    —*a cross-curriculum connection*

    —*an extension into the reader's own life*

- Post-reading Activities

- Culminating Activities

- Three Different Options for Unit Tests

- Bibliography of Related Reading

- Answer Key

We are confident that this unit will be a valuable addition to your literature planning, and that as you use our ideas, your students will learn to treasure the stories to which you introduce them.

Sample Lesson Plan

Each of the lessons suggested below can take from one to several days to complete.

Lesson 1
- Introduce and complete some or all of the pre-reading activities. (page 5)
- Read About the Author with your students. (page 6)
- Read the book summary with your students. (page 7)
- Introduce Section 1 vocabulary words. (page 8)

Lesson 2
- Read chapters 1 through 8. As you read, place the vocabulary words in the context of the story and discuss their meanings.
- Complete a vocabulary activity. (page 9)
- Design a dream bedroom. (page 11)
- Complete Stately Knowledge activity. (pages 12 and 13)
- Practice using pronouns correctly. (page 14)
- Write about changes in life. (page 15)
- Administer the Section 1 quiz. (page 10)
- Introduce Section 2 vocabulary words. (page 8)

Lesson 3
- Read chapters 9 through 15. As you read, place the vocabulary words in context and discuss their meanings.
- Complete a vocabulary activity. (page 9)
- Write a declaration of war. (page 17)
- Make a mini-book research report about the American Revolution. (pages 18 and 19)
- Collect data about favorite games of classmates and make a graph. (page 20)
- Discuss peer pressure. (page 21)
- Administer the Section 2 quiz. (page 16)
- Introduce Section 3 vocabulary words. (page 8)

Lesson 4
- Read chapters 16 through 22. As you read, place the vocabulary words in context and discuss their meanings.
- Complete a vocabulary activity. (page 9)
- Learn about the flags of the American Revolution. (page 23 and 24)
- Go on a shopping spree. (page 25)
- Search for the correct synonyms. (page 26)
- Write a poem about a special person. (page 27)

- Administer the Section 3 quiz. (page 22)
- Introduce Section 4 vocabulary words. (page 8)

Lesson 5
- Read chapters 23 through 30. As you read, place the vocabulary words in context and discuss their meanings.
- Complete a vocabulary activity. (page 9)
- Make some Fancy Fish. (page 29)
- Research Facts About Fish. (page 30)
- Make a mini-book about fish. (page 31)
- Label the parts of a fish. (page 32)
- Write a postcard to someone special. (page 33)
- Administer the Section 4 quiz. (page 28)
- Introduce Section 5 vocabulary words. (page 8)

Lesson 6
- Read chapters 31 through 37. As you read, place the vocabulary words in the context of the story and discuss their meanings.
- Complete a vocabulary activity. (page 9)
- Make a Splash Art door sign. (page 35)
- Do a character analysis of Peter and Grandpa. (page 36)
- Complete the Crossword Puzzle. (page 37)
- Think about how an event in your life has affected you and others. (page 38)
- Administer the Section 5 quiz. (page 34)

Lesson 7
- Assign work on Similes. (page 39)
- Discuss any questions students may have about the story. (page 40)
- Assign one or more of the Potpourri of Possibilities. (page 40)
- Work on the culminating activities. (pages 41–42)

Lesson 8
- Administer one or more of the unit tests. (pages 43–45)
- Discuss the test answers. (page 48)
- Provide lists of related reading and Web sites for students. (page 46)

Before the Book

Before you begin reading *The War with Grandpa* with your students, complete some of the following discussions and activities to stimulate their interest in the book.

1. Predict what the story might be about by hearing the title.

2. Predict what the story might be about by looking at the cover illustration.

3. Discuss other books written by Robert Kimmel Smith that students may have read.

Chocolate Fever

Mostly Michael

Jelly Belly

Squeaky Wheel

Bobby Baseball

4. Ask students to give their definitions of the word "family."

5. Ask students if they have any relatives who have fought in any wars.

6. Invite a grandparent to the classroom to talk about his or her life and the changes the grandparent has seen and experienced over the years.

7. Ask students the following questions:

   • Do you have your own room?

   • Would you like to move out of your bedroom to another room in your house?

   • Do you have any grandparents living with you?

   • Have you ever been angry with someone you care about deeply?

   • Have you ever done anything that you have regretted?

   • Would you ever

      —be influenced by peers to do something you might not be sure of?

      —spend an entire day with an enemy?

      —play mean tricks on a member of your family?

About the Author

Robert Kimmel Smith was born on July 31, 1930, in Brooklyn, New York. At the age of eight, he read his first book, *Toby Tyler*, which brought tears to his eyes. After that, he always dreamed about being a writer.

As Smith grew, he enjoyed reading about the Wild West, pioneers, and pirates. When he was a teenager, he told his parents that he wished to become a writer. Because it was during the Depression, his parents told him, "There is no way you can make a living," and they convinced him to go into medicine.

Smith was discontented with college so he left and was drafted by the United States Army. He was discharged from the Army in 1953, and he went back to New York where he met Claire Medney, whom he married the following year.

Smith began writing short stories while working for an advertising agency in New York. These initial writing experiences gave him a taste of dealing with the demands that are placed on a writer. Smith says, "You don't write a book in one day. In fact, the mere thought of writing a whole book is sort of staggering. But, if you can write five good pages a day (and you can), then pretty soon you have a book."

Eventually, Smith got away from the advertising business and began a career as a full-time writer. He gives credit to his daughter, Heidi, for getting him started on his first book in 1970. *Chocolate Fever* began as a bedtime story that Smith made up for Heidi. It was about a boy who loved chocolate, and that boy was Smith himself. He continued the story every night, and after it ended, Heidi wanted to hear it again. So Smith "wrote it all out." *Chocolate Fever* went on to sell about two million copies.

Ideas for Smith's books usually come from his own life experiences or from experiences of people he knows. Smith's philosophy is to "write funny about serious things." He states, "Underneath the humor, there's serious stuff. I just don't get it too close to the surface." *Jelly Belly*, published in 1981, is about Smith's own childhood as a fat kid. He calls this his "funniest book" and says, "I get mail from kids who say it's the funniest book they've ever read." Smith's son, Roger, was the main inspiration to write *The War with Grandpa*. Roger "loved his room, and he never wanted to live anywhere else." Peter, the main character in the story, also loves his room. However, his grandfather comes to live with Peter's family and moves into Peter's room. Peter declares war on his grandpa in an attempt to regain control of his room and does things his parents have forbidden him to do. *The War with Grandpa* is "an honest tale of a painful family adjustment process."

Other stories written by Smith from personal experiences include *Mostly Michael*, written in diary form through the eyes of an eleven-year-old boy, Bobby Baseball and inspired by his son's Little League team and *Squeaky Wheel*, which is about divorce.

Note: References for this biographical sketch are from *Something About the Author*, Volume 77, pages 196–200.

The War with Grandpa

by Robert Kimmel Smith

(Dell Publishing Company, 1984)

(Available in Canada, Doubleday Dell Seal; UK, Bantam Doubleday Dell; AUS, Transworld Publishers)

Peter Stokes is in the fifth grade, and his English assignment is to write a story about an event in his life that is true and real. Peter decides to write about when he and his grandfather went to war with each other.

Peter loves his Grandpa Jack who lives in Florida. But since Grandma died, Grandpa Jack has been very lonely. He decides to sell his house and move in with Peter's family. When Grandpa arrives, he mopes a great deal and does not seem to have energy to do anything. His spirits are low.

Because Grandpa Jack has a bad leg and has difficulty going up and down stairs, Peter's parents move Peter out of the room he loves and has lived in all his life to a new, scary room on the third floor. Grandpa takes over Peter's room. Peter thinks this is very unfair, and at the urging of two of his friends, Steve and Billy, declares war on his grandpa. He is determined to get his room back.

Peter writes a declaration of war to his grandpa, stating his demands. Grandpa ignores the note so Peter makes his first attack. He sets Grandpa's alarm clock for 3:00 A.M. After meeting under a flag of truce and accomplishing nothing, Peter makes his second attack. He steals Grandpa's slippers. Now, Grandpa is ready to fight back, and he makes a counterattack. He hides all the pieces to Peter's Monopoly game.

Even though Peter and his grandpa are in the middle of a war, they decide to go fishing for the first time together. This day becomes a very special memory for Peter, and he realizes how deep his feelings are for his grandpa. However, the war continues, and Peter steals Grandpa's wristwatch in his next attack. As Grandpa makes his counterattacks, his spirits begin to lift, and he sees that the war is helping him get over his sadness.

However, Peter's last attack proves to be a little too cruel. He steals Grandpa's false teeth, feels awful about what he has done, surrenders, and apologizes to Grandpa. They both realize that war only hurts and wounds people, especially those you love.

After the war is over, Grandpa, with Peter's help, fixes the basement for himself. Dad's office gets moved to the third floor, and Peter gets his old room back.

Vocabulary Lists

On this page are the vocabulary lists which correspond to each sectional grouping of chapters as outlined in the Table of Contents. Activities that reinforce the vocabulary words can be found on page 9 of this book.

Section One *(Chapters 1–8)*

billboard	hair net	Hank Aaron	intensity
maniac	flickered	John Paul Jones	venetian blinds
rickety	advantage	fixture	taxes
ballet	formica	accountant	floorboards
respect	ledger	solemn	attitude

Section Two *(Chapters 9–15)*

emphysema	peppy	guerrilla warfare	Redcoats
arthritis	fanatic	declaration	Minutemen
pirouette	wishy-washy	construction	identity
depressed	conceal	invading	Revolution
mope	peasants	Yankees	warrior

Section Three *(Chapters 16–22)*

kin	annoy	protests	single-minded
surrenders	dispute	Pearl Harbor	chuckling
monkeyshines	mussed	index cards	truce
revealing	digital	underestimate	
meander	unnatural	retire	

Section Four *(Chapters 23–30)*

applauded	olfactory	casual	dominoes
grudge	sarcastic	diabolical	campaign
tutu	repeg	asterisk	succeed
obnoxious	flounder	peculiar	encore
tantrum	vinyl	mystified	tides

Section Five *(Chapters 31–37)*

revenge	massive	flannel	garment bag
retaliation	ducts	translated	enlarge
paneling	liverwurst	moonlighting	
indubitably	dingy	panic	

8

Vocabulary Activity Ideas

You can help your students learn and retain the vocabulary in *The War with Grandpa* by providing them with interesting vocabulary ideas. Here are a few ideas to try.

❑ Ask students to make their own **Word Search Puzzles** from graph paper, using the vocabulary words on page 8.

❑ Have students play **Vocabulary Concentration**. The goal of this game is to match vocabulary words with their definitions. Make two sets of cards that are the same size and color. On one set, write the vocabulary words. On the other set, write the matching definitions. As students begin to play, all cards are mixed together and placed facedown on a desk or table. The first player picks two cards. If the pair matches the word with its definition, the player keeps the cards. If the cards do not match, they are returned to their place on the table facedown. The game continues until all matches have been made. The player with the most matches is the winner.

❑ As a small group activity, have students work together to create **Picture Dictionaries** of the vocabulary words.

❑ Hand out blank Bingo cards to students to play **Vocabulary Bingo**. Have them place one vocabulary word in each space on the card. Students may place the words in any order on their cards. Then randomly pick and read the vocabulary definitions. A student wins by covering a row on his or her card diagonally, vertically, or horizontally.

❑ Make group **Vocabulary Stories**. Have two to four students in a group write on any subject and include at least 10 words from any of the vocabulary words listed on page 8.

❑ Challenge students to find **Antonyms** or **Synonyms** for the vocabulary words for each section.

❑ Have your students write **Word Letters**. Ask each student to pick a partner and write a letter to that partner. Then, have the partner write a response. Give the students one point for every vocabulary word they can use in their letters and replies.

❑ For each vocabulary section on page 8, create a **Funny Font Vocabulary Puzzle**. Select a font such as Dingbats or Wingdings that prints symbols in place of letters. Type the alphabet in symbols across the top of a page and type the vocabulary words for that section below it. Leave space for the students to decipher each one correctly.

❑ Have students create their own **Mixed-up Words Game**. Have student teams scramble and rewrite words for other student teams to unscramble.

❑ Prepare a list of **Vocabulary Definitions** from page 8. Set up a station with a rubber-stamp set of the alphabet and have students stamp the matching vocabulary words in their free time.

❑ Have your students practice their writing skills by creating sentences and paragraphs in which multiple vocabulary words are used correctly. Ask them to share their **Power Vocabulary** sentences and paragraphs with the class.

Quiz Time!

1. On the back of this paper, list three main events of this section. Then answer the rest of the questions on this page.

2. Why do you think the first chapter is called "Peter Stokes' True and Real Story"?

_____

_____

3. What does Jennifer like best in life?

_____

4. Why is Grandpa Jack coming to live at Peter's house?

_____

_____

5. Jenny says she loves Grandpa "up to the sky and down to the ocean." What does she mean?

_____

6. Why couldn't Jennifer move into a new room instead of Peter?

_____

_____

7. Based on the contents of Peter's toy cabinet, what do you think Peter likes to do?

_____

_____

8. What is the last thing to be moved into Peter's new room?

_____

9. Describe how Peter's new room is different from his old room.

_____

_____

_____

10. What is Peter thinking about when he finally falls asleep during the first night in his new room?

_____

_____

10

Designing a Dream Bedroom

Peter loves his bedroom. He has lived there his whole life and does not want to move to a different room. If you could design a "dream bedroom," what would it look like? What would a person see when he opened the door to your room? Design your dream bedroom by following the directions below. When you finish, write a descriptive paragraph about your room, using the paragraph starter provided.

Materials

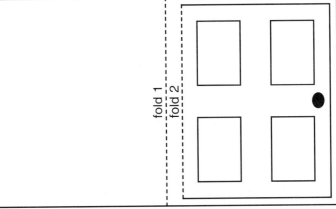

- one piece of 12" x 18" (30 cm x 46 cm) construction paper
- ruler
- scissors
- glue
- crayons, markers, or colored pencils

Procedure

1. Fold the piece of construction paper in half. (See fold 1, above.)

2. Draw a door that almost fills the front right of the paper.

3. Cut along the top, the right side, and the bottom of the door, and fold it back along fold 2 so the door opens.

4. Glue the front edges around the door opening to the other half of the paper as it is folded back.

5. Draw your dream bedroom on the paper behind the door.

Let me tell you about my room! I love it!_____

_____

_____

_____

_____

_____

_____

_____

Stately Knowledge

Grandpa Jack lives in Florida before he comes to live with Peter's family. Even though we do not know where Peter lives, every state, including his, has its own special history and its own special facts. With a partner research your state on the Internet by typing in the following address:

http://www.ipl.org/youth/stateknow/

When you arrive at this site, use the arrow on the right side of the screen to scroll down the page until you are able to click on the name of your state. As you reach the page you have been linked to, again use the arrow on the right side of the screen to scroll down and read to fill in the following information about your state. (**Note:** If you have no access to the Internet or have difficulty finding the address, use traditional sources.)

Capital _____

Population_____

Governor_____

Motto _____

Nickname _____

Flower_____

Bird_____

Song _____

Entered the Union on_____as the _____state.

Major industries _____

_____

List at least three points of interest._____

_____

_____

Now use the map on page 13 to complete the following tasks.

- Locate and label your state with its proper abbreviation.
- Color your state.
- Locate and label its capital city.
- Locate and label the states that border your state with their proper abbreviations.
- Draw a compass rose on the map.
- Locate and label the five Great Lakes.
- Locate and label the Atlantic Ocean, the Gulf of Mexico, and the Pacific Ocean.

Stately Knowledge *(cont.)*

See page 12 for directions.

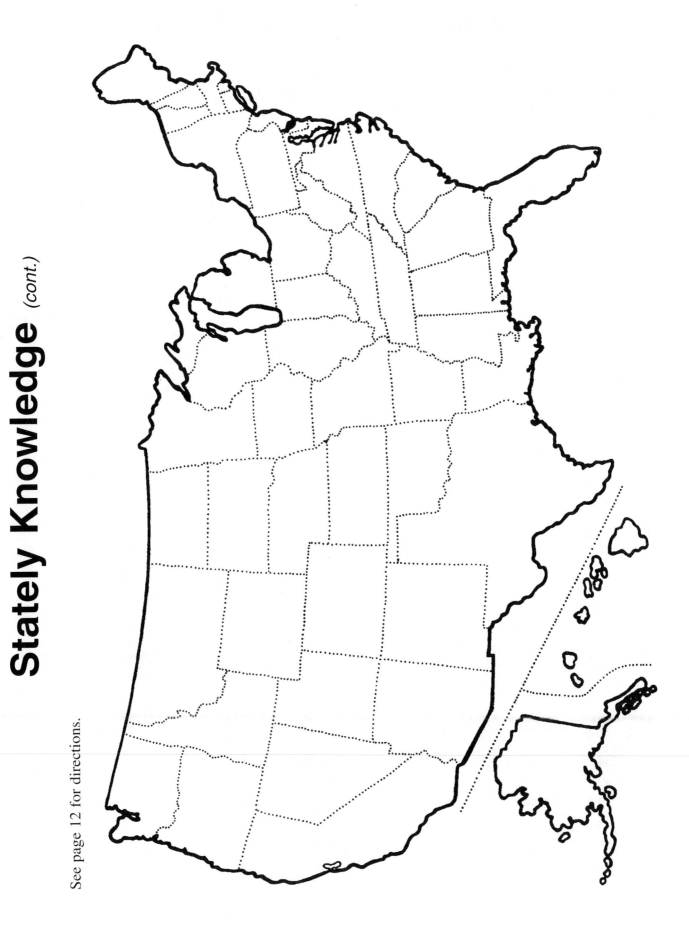

Positively Pronouns

A subject pronoun takes the place of one or more words in the subject of a sentence. Words such as *I, you, he, she, it, we,* and *they* are subject pronouns. Read the following sentences from Chapters 1–8 and then replace the underlined word or words with a subject pronoun.

1. <u>Peter</u> is typing his story on his dad's typewriter.   _____

2. <u>Jennifer</u> just came in and asked what I was doing.   _____

3. <u>The story</u> is about what happened when Grandpa came to live with us.   _____

4. <u>Jenny</u> is very beautiful with long blond hair and lovely blue eyes.   _____

5. <u>The rocker</u> used to be in the living room.   _____

6. <u>My mom and dad</u> brought the rocker up to my room.   _____

7. <u>Jenny and I</u> are supposed to cheer up Grandpa when he comes.   _____

8. "For once you found out a good secret, Jenny," <u>Peter</u> said.   _____

9. <u>Peter</u> picked up the book on my bed and began reading.   _____

10. <u>Grandpa Jack</u> is too lonely down in Florida since Grandma died.   _____

11. <u>Peter</u> has lived in this room all his life.   _____

12. <u>The yellow toy cabinets</u> have all my stuff in them.   _____

13. <u>My desk</u> is in the corner where my crib used to be.   _____

14. <u>Grandpa Jack and Jenny</u> don't live in my room.   _____

15. "<u>Jennifer</u> can't tell you the secret," Jennifer said.   _____

16. Will <u>Grandpa Jack</u> play the piano for me while I dance?   _____

17. Mom said, "<u>Dad and I</u> have some wonderful news for you."   _____

18. "Couldn't <u>Dad</u> put a shower in the top floor bathroom?" I said to Dad.   _____

19. <u>Mom and Dad</u> couldn't move Jenny upstairs because she was still a baby.   _____

20. <u>Dad and I</u> didn't want to talk about it anymore.   _____

Changes in Life

Peter's grandfather is coming to live with Peter's family. This will bring about some changes for everyone. What are some of the changes that have occurred in your life? Were they positive or negative experiences for you? Get into groups of three or four students. During the first 10 minutes, record on the chart below the changes that have occurred in your own life and also whether these changes were positive or negative. Then share your responses with other members of your group.

Change That Occurred	Positive/Negative

Quiz Time!

1. On the back of this paper, list three main events of this section. Then answer the rest of the questions on this page.

2. How did Peter's grandma die?_____

3. What does Peter mean when he describes his grandparents, using the simile, "They were a pair, like shoes or gloves"?

   _____

   _____

4. What is wrong with Grandpa's leg?

   _____

5. Mom describes Grandpa as "not having any life in him." What does she mean?

   _____

   _____

6. According to Peter, what does Grandpa do when he mopes?

   _____

7. What does Mom mean when she says, "Only a dope will mope"?

   _____

   _____

8. Steve is a Risk fanatic. What does this mean? Are you a fanatic about anything?

   _____

   _____

9. Based on the description of Peter's friends Steve and Billy, which one is more like yourself and why?

   _____

   _____

   _____

10. What is Peter's first step in starting the war, and what is Grandpa's reaction to it?

   _____

   _____

Declaration of War!

When Peter writes his declaration of war to his grandpa, he makes it known that they are going to war over Peter's bedroom. Imagine that you are Peter. What would you write in your declaration of war? Use this page to write your declaration. Share your declaration with other classmates.

Revolutionary Pursuit

Before Peter makes his declaration of war, he begins to think about what Steve had said about the Revolutionary days. The American Revolution began in 1775 between the 13 American colonies and England. The colonists wanted independence, or freedom, from England. The king was like a father to the people who fought in the American Revolution, and Peter compares his own situation to this war.

For this activity, you will write a research report. With a group of two or three people, research one of the following words and phrases relating to the American Revolution.

- Battles of Lexington and Concord
- Valley Forge
- Minutemen
- Paul Revere
- Thomas Paine
- Continental Congress
- Boston Tea Party

- George Washington
- Thomas Gage
- Stamp Act
- Declaration of Independence
- Battle of Bunker Hill
- The Treaty of Paris
- The Proclamation of 1763

Write the topic you chose here: _____

Use several sources, including the Internet, computer software programs, and book reference, to complete your research on the topic you chose. (**Note:** Be sure you have permission to use the Internet or computer software before using them.)

For information found on a computer source, answer the following questions:

- What Internet addresses did you locate? List two addresses. _____

  _____

- What features are available on the Internet site(s) you found?_____

  _____

- What computer software did you use? _____

  _____

- Does the software you used provide an interactive program?_____

Using your book or computer sources, select the most important information you will use to report on your topic. Use the space below and the back of this paper to plan your research report.

_____

_____

_____

Prepare a report booklet using the forms on page 19. The form at the top will be your report cover. Reproduce as many copies of the bottom as you need to write your report. Assemble the report pages to complete your report booklet.

Revolutionary Pursuit (cont.)

The Revolutionary War

A Report By

_____

_____

_____

_____

_____

_____

_____

_____

_____

_____

_____

_____

Playing Games

Steve is a Risk fanatic. Peter likes to play Monopoly and Clue. Ask classmates to think collectively of six favorite board games. List these on the back of this paper and also write them below the six columns on the graph. Then collect data in tally form from individuals about their favorite board games and keep track of this information on the back. After you have collected the data, put it into the bar graph. Think of an appropriate title for your graph.

20						
19						
18						
17						
16						
15						
14						
13						
12						
11						
10						
9						
8						
7						
6						
5						
4						
3						
2						
1						
0						

____ ____ ____ ____ ____ ____

The Pressure Is On!

Peter, Billy, and Steve have been friends since they met in kindergarten. Despite their differences, they get along well and visit each other's homes. After Grandpa moves in, Steve and Billy call Peter's grandpa a "room robber" and believe that Peter should put up a fight to get his room back.

Do you think Peter is influenced by his friends to start the war with Grandpa? Have you ever been influenced by peer pressure? In the chart below, list any times in your life that peer pressure may have influenced your decision to do things that you were not sure you wanted to do. Then answer the questions.

Pressure!
1.
2.
3.
4.
5.

Is there any way to resist pressures from peers and still maintain friendships?

_____

_____

_____

Are there any types of friendships that are not worth saving because of peer pressure?

_____

_____

_____

Quiz Time!

1. On the back of this paper, list three main events of this section. Then answer the rest of the questions on this page.

2. What do Billy and Steve think about starting a war with a note? _____

   _____

3. Describe Peter's first attack plan. _____

   _____

4. How does Grandpa react to the first attack? _____

   _____

5. Grandpa tells Peter, "You don't go to war against kin." What does he mean? _____

   _____

   _____

6. Describe Peter's second attack. _____

   _____

   _____

7. Why do you think Peter spells the word *defeated* incorrectly on the note he leaves for Grandpa during his second attack?

   _____

   _____

8. What mistake does Peter make during his second attack? _____

   _____

9. How does Peter feel about his grandpa even though he is having a war with him?

   _____

   _____

10. Why does Grandpa slap Peter's cheek? _____

    _____

Flags Worth Flying

Grandpa and Peter put up a flag of truce after Peter's first attack so they can meet to talk things out. A flag of truce is a white flag, which is a sign to warring parties that there is a cease-fire.

Typically, the most important use of a flag is as an emblem of a nation or state. Using a printed or electronic source, do some research about the flags of the American Revolution. Illustrate the flag of the 13 Colonies and the British flag. Describe the meaning behind any symbols on each flag.

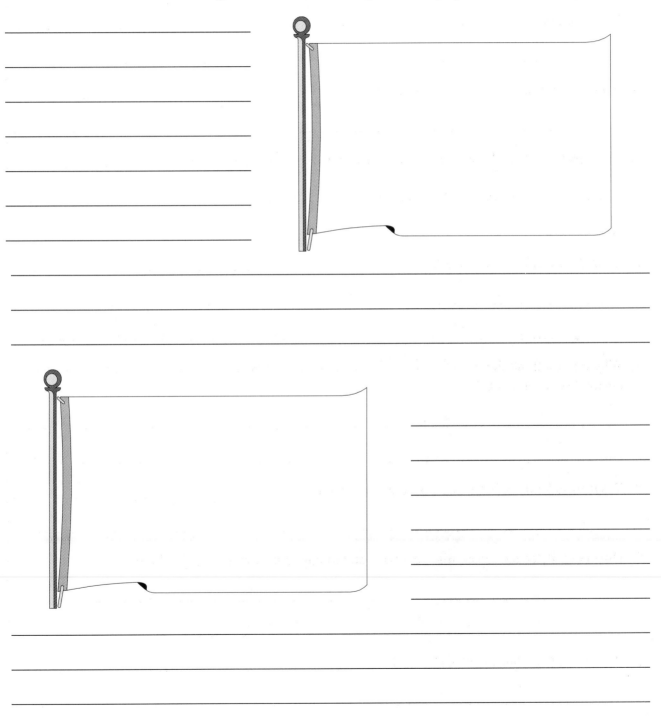

Flags Worth Flying *(cont.)*

Betsy Ross sewed the first flag for the United States. The answers to the following questions are found on The Betsy Ross Home Page on the Internet at this address:

http://www.libertynet.org/iha/betsy/index.html

When you arrive at this page, the links are in the shape of a flag. After reading the questions, decide which link to click on to find the answers. (**Note:** If you have no access to the Internet or have difficulty finding the address, use traditional sources.)

1. Who asked Betsy Ross to sew the first flag for the United States? _____

   _____

2. Who cut the American flag into pieces and was honored for doing it? _____

   _____

3. Is it ever appropriate to fly the flag upside down? _____

   _____

4. What is done with worn or outdated flags?_____

   _____

5. What is a vexillologist? _____

6. In what year did Francis Scott Key write "The Star-Spangled Banner"?_____

7. What two states were the last to enter the Union, and in what years did they enter?

   _____

8. By 1818, the Union consisted of 20 states. A law was made that stated the flag would have 13 stripes and that every time a state was added to the Union, a star would be added. However, no law was made as to the arrangement of stripes, so at this time in history, there were three different arrangements. Draw these three flags below.

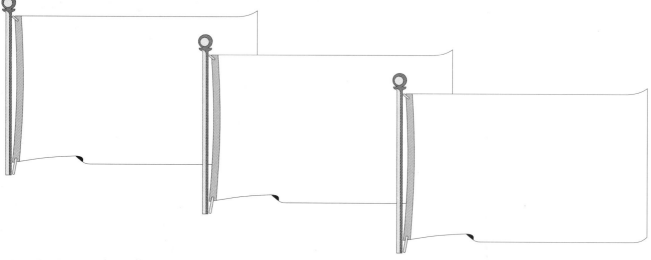

Shopping Spree

Steve, Billy, and Peter go shopping at Dealtown because Steve needs school supplies. With two classmates, imagine that you are going shopping at a store in your city to purchase school supplies. You and your classmates have $45.00 to spend at the store. Create a detailed list, showing how you and your classmates would spend the money. The chart below shows the items available for purchase and their prices. Your goal is to try to spend as close to $45.00 as possible without going over. There is no limit on amounts purchased; however, at least five different items must be purchased by each classmate.

School Supplies Price List	
5 ballpoint pens	$ .89
12 pencils	$ .79
50 index cards	$1.29
80 page spiral notebook	$1.19
marker set	$2.99
3 ring binder	$3.29
colored pencil pack	$1.39
scissors	$2.19
2 pocket folders	$ .29
10 high density disks	$6.99

Write your detailed list in the table below. Continue on the back of this paper if necessary.

Consumer	Item	Quantity	Cost

Searching for Synonyms

When Grandpa and Peter take a walk because they have some talking to do, Grandpa uses the word "dispute" in place of "disagreement." Words that have the same or nearly the same meaning are called *synonyms*.

Two of the three words in each row below are synonyms. Find the two words that are synonyms and circle them.

1.	disagreement	dispute	meeting
2.	agile	fumble	blunder
3.	warrior	doctor	soldier
4.	kin	family	stranger
5.	prepare	break	fix
6.	stare	meander	roam
7.	stubborn	friendly	bullheaded
8.	attack	surrender	give up
9.	quit	retire	work
10.	bother	annoy	like
11.	chuckle	laugh	cry
12.	cease-fire	argue	truce
13.	coats	capers	monkeyshines
14.	elders	teenagers	seniors
15.	tease	respect	admire
16.	foe	friend	enemy
17.	devious	honest	sneaky
18.	mistake	plan	strategy
19.	abnormal	unnatural	usual
20.	feud	friendship	fight

Special People Poetry

Peter tells his grandpa, "I love you, but the war is still on!" after their first peace conference. Peter has deep feelings for his grandpa despite the fact that they are involved in a war.

Think of a grandparent or someone close to you and write a cinquain about that person. A **cinquain** is a five-line poem with the following pattern:

> *line 1:* noun
> *line 2:* two adjectives describing the noun
> *line 3:* three verbs showing actions of the noun
> *line 4:* four-word phrase telling about the noun
> *line 5:* repeat noun from line one or a synonym

Quiz Time!

1. On the back of this paper, list three main events of this section. Then answer the rest of the questions on this page.

2. What happens during the first lull of the war? _____

   _____

3. Describe Grandpa's first counterattack._____

   _____

   _____

4. How does Grandpa sign his note to Peter? _____

5. How do the boys react to each other after Grandpa's first counterattack?

   _____

   _____

6. If Peter and Grandpa are at war, why does Grandpa fix Peter's rocker? _____

   _____

7. Describe how the war is affecting Grandpa's attitude about life. _____

   _____

   _____

8. What does Grandpa teach Peter while they are fighting? _____

   _____

   _____

9. If Peter has such a good day with Grandpa, why does he feel so sad later that night?

   _____

   _____

10. How does Grandpa get his watch back, and how does Peter get his Monopoly game back?

   _____

   _____

Fancy Fish

Peter and Grandpa go fishing for flounder near the ocean. A flounder is a type of fish that has special coloring, called camouflage, to help it hide from enemies. A flounder will blend with the bottom of the ocean because it is not very colorful.

Imagine what a fish would look like if its surroundings were beautiful ocean flowers with many colors! To get an idea of the camouflage that this type of fish would need, cut out the outline of the fish below. Next, cut your fish into three pieces, any sizes or shapes. Label the back of each piece with your initials. Your teacher will collect all the pieces from everyone in your class and randomly hand three pieces back to everyone. If someone gets his initialed piece, he or she will trade with someone else. Color the three pieces you have been given on the side without the initials, using any colors or any designs. Then, return the colored pieces to their owners. Next, find the people who have colored your three pieces and fit them together to see your fancy fish! Glue your fish onto a large sheet of construction paper, and add an ocean life background.

Facts About Fish

Peter had never been fishing before. Grandpa taught him many things about fishing during the day they spent together. Do some research about fish on the Internet by typing in this address:

http://www.wh.whoi.edu/faq.index.html

When you arrive at this site, use the arrow on the right side of the screen to scroll down this page to find answers to questions 1–15. When you have finished your research, make a little book by following the directions on the next page. Summarize your research from the Internet in your little book of Fish Facts. (**Note:** If you have no access to the Internet or if you have difficulty finding the address, use traditional sources.)

1. How many fish species are there? _____

2. What is the world's largest fish? _____

3. What is the world's smallest fish? _____

4. What is the most common fish in the sea? _____

5. Describe how fish sleep. _____

   _____

6. What is an anadromous fish? _____

   _____

7. What is a catadromous fish? _____

   _____

8. How is the age of a fish determined? _____

   _____

9. How long do fish live? _____

10. What is the term used for fish who give birth to living young? _____

11. Do fish breathe? _____

12. How fast can fish swim? _____

13. Can fish swim backwards? _____

14. Do all fish swim in the horizontal position? _____

15. Why don't fish chew their food? _____

   _____

Facts About Fish *(cont.)*

Follow these simple steps to make your mini-book about fish facts.

1. Find a standard-size sheet of paper.

2. Make the folds as indicated by the dotted lines below.

3. Unfold and refold, as shown. Then, make a cut on the solid line through two thicknesses.

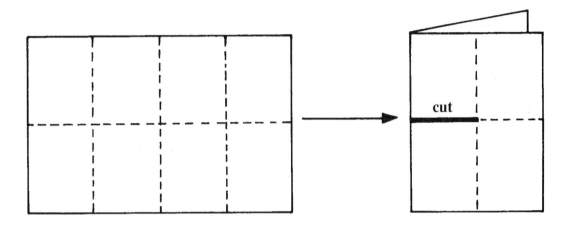

4. Next, open the folded paper after you have made the cut and refold it lengthwise.

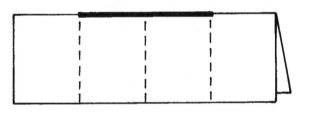

5. Push the two ends together, fold, and close your book.

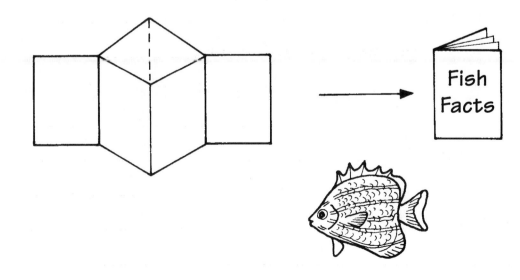

Fish Parts

The only time Peter had ever seen a live fish was in a big tank at a store. Fish have many parts to their bodies, just as humans do. Fish, however, have different types of fins for movement instead of arms or legs. Do some research in an encyclopedia or a science book that tells about parts of a fish. Locate and label the following parts:

- scales
- gill opening
- eye
- soft dorsal fin
- spiny dorsal fin
- mouth
- caudal fin
- anal fin
- pectoral fin
- pelvic fin

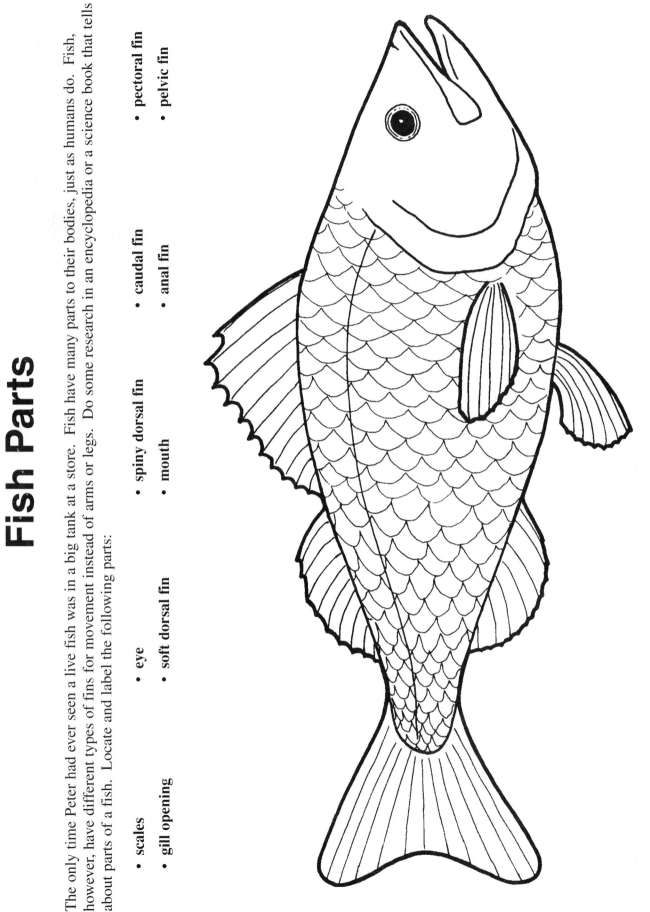

Writing a Postcard

The day that Peter spent with Grandpa was very special to him. Think about a time that you spent with someone special. On the lines below, write some of your thoughts about your time together. It could have been for only a few hours, an entire day, or a whole week. Use your notes to write a postcard to that person, telling him or her how you felt about the time the two of you spent together. Decorate your postcard and mail it!

_____
name of person

_____

_____

_____

_____

_____

_____

Place stamp
here.

Quiz Time!

1. On the back of this paper, list three main events of this section. Then answer the rest of the questions on this page.

2. Why is chapter 31 called "The Shoe Drops . . . Kerplunk"? _____
   _____

3. List the nine tricks involved in Grandpa's revenge. _____
   _____

   _____

   _____

   _____

4. How do Steve and Billy react when Peter tells them about Grandpa's revenge? _____
   _____

5. What does Peter do for his revenge? _____
   _____

6. How does Grandpa feel when Peter steals his teeth? _____

7. Why does Peter give Grandpa his teeth back so quickly? _____
   _____

8. There is one reason why Grandpa thinks the war is somewhat fun. What is it?
   _____

   _____

9. What does Grandpa think should have happened before Peter's parents took his room away from him?
   _____

   _____

10. Describe how the conflict that started the war between Peter and Grandpa is resolved.
    _____

    _____

Splash Art

After Peter moves back into his old room, he feels like he has not felt for a long time. As he is lying on his bed, he hears a loud banging noise on the outside of his door. Grandpa has made a wooden sign for Peter's room and is hanging it on his door.

Follow the directions below to make a sign for your room.

Materials

- 9" x 9" (23 cm x 23 cm) piece of white construction paper

- tempera paint

- 10" x 10" (25 cm x 25 cm) colored construction paper

- 3" x 5" (8 cm x 13 cm) blank index paper

- marker or crayons

- glue

- newspaper (to cover working surface)

- drinking straw

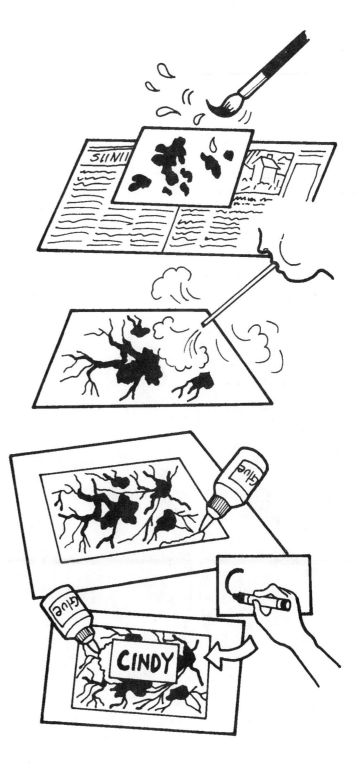

Directions

1. Place the white construction paper on newspaper.

2. Splash paint droplets on the paper.

3. Blow through a straw to spread the paint around. Allow the paint to dry.

4. Place the splash art (white construction paper square) on top of the colored construction paper square so that the larger square looks like a frame for the art piece. Glue the two pieces together.

5. Use a marker or crayon to write your name on the blank index card.

6. Glue the index paper to the center of the splash art picture.

Characterization

Peter and Grandpa display different characteristics throughout the story. For example, Peter knows that Grandpa is lonely because he holds a photograph of Grandma in his hands and does not even hear Peter say good night. Sometimes we can tell things about people from the way they act or the things they say and do. With a partner, complete the character diagrams about Peter and Grandpa. List some characteristics and examples in the diagram below. Be ready to share your diagram with the rest of the class.

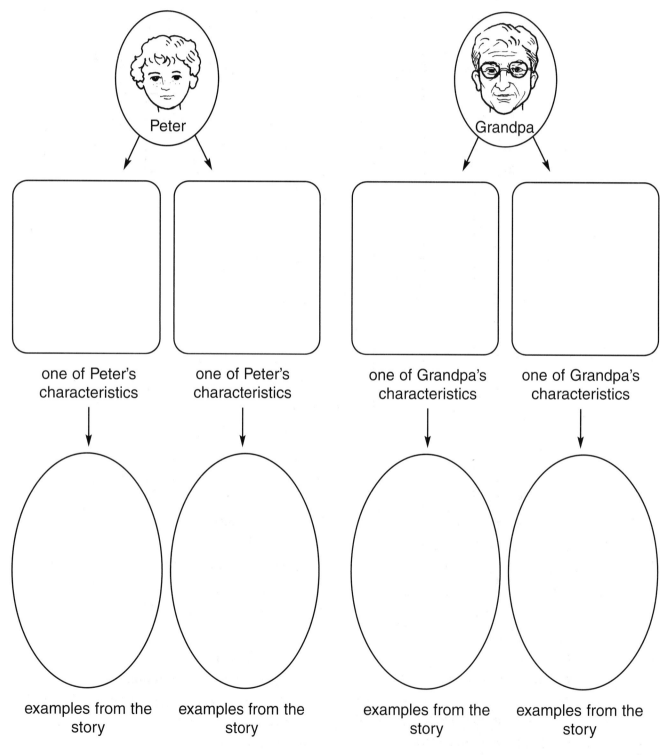

| one of Peter's characteristics | one of Peter's characteristics | one of Grandpa's characteristics | one of Grandpa's characteristics |

| examples from the story | examples from the story | examples from the story | examples from the story |

Crossword Puzzle

Read the clues and complete the crossword puzzle.

Across

4. Grandpa was known as the_____ _____.
6. what Peter took in his last attack
9. the first name of Peter's dad
11. the grade Peter will be in next year
12. Only a dope will do this.
15. This was missing money, playing pieces, properties, and rules.
16. person who has excessive enthusiasm about something
17. Steve is an expert at this game.
18. Grandpa used to live in this state.
19. Peter was known as the Secret_____.

Down

1. Jenny wears a tutu while doing_____.
2. loves horses a lot
3. Fish like to feed at this time.
5. synonym for dispute
7. Grandma died from_____.
8. fiendish
9. disturb or irritate
10. agreement to halt fighting
13. the business Grandpa had been in before he retired
14. get revenge

Events of Life

The war between Grandpa and Peter affects them in different ways. For Grandpa, the war lifts his spirits, but in the end he is hurt when Peter steals his false teeth. Because of the war, Peter begins to think about his life at a deeper level. He begins to think about peer pressure and how he must decide for himself what is right or wrong. He also realizes that he enjoys writing.

Think of an event in your own life and how it affected you and other people who may have been involved. Fill in the diagram and share it with the class, if you wish.

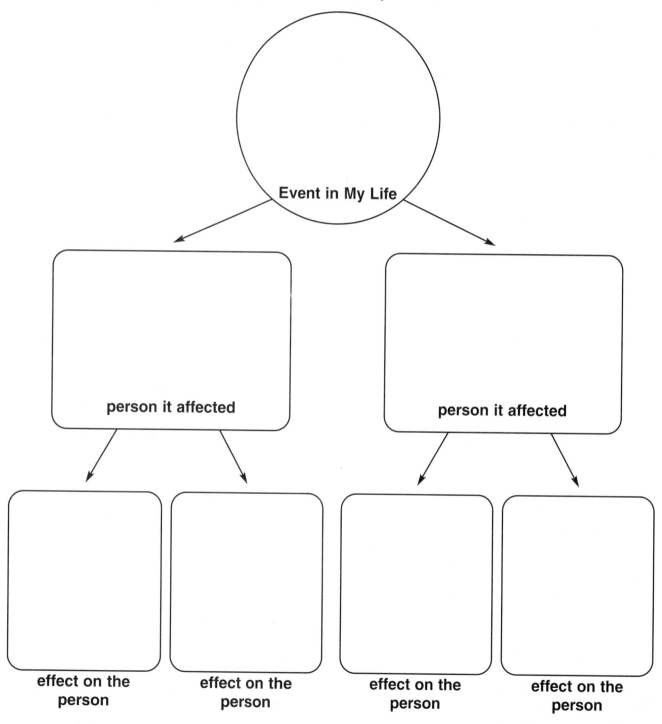

Similes

Robert Kimmel Smith uses figurative language to make his writing more interesting for his readers. A **simile** is one type of figurative language which compares two things, usually unlike each other, using the words *like* or *as*. For example, in chapter five there is the sentence, "Meanwhile, I was as sad as I ever was, up in my room, and about as blue as the sky." In this case, Peter's mood is being compared to a blue sky so the reader can feel how sad he really is.

With a partner, find the following similes in *The War with Grandpa*. Figure out what things or people the author is comparing and why the comparison is being made. (**Note:** Page numbers refer to the book edtion used for this unit.)

1. *She looked like a walking billboard.* (page 2) _____
   _____

2. *"That's not the secret," she said, putting her hand on her hip and posing like a statue or something.* (page 7)_____
   _____

3. *I jumped up from my chair, ran up to my room, threw myself on the bed, and cried like a maniac.* (page 16) _____
   _____

4. *With open doors to empty rooms that looked like black caves where someone could be hiding.* (page 27) _____
   _____

5. *They were a pair, like shoes or gloves.* (page 31) _____
   _____

6. *"Petey, you're springing up like a weed."* (page 31) _____
   _____

7. *I sneaked down the hallway like a thief in the night.* (page 55)_____
   _____

8. *I would have to be as mean as Darth Vader to hate him.* (page 75) _____
   _____

9. *"Got it," Grandpa said, "solid as the Rock of Gibraltar."* (page 90)_____
   _____

10. *The stars looked like asterisks.* (page 96) _____
    _____

Potpourri of Possibilities

Do some or all of the following activities after you finish reading *The War with Grandpa*.

Any Questions?

Did you have questions that were left unanswered at the end of the story? Write some of your questions here.

_____

_____

_____

Work in groups or by yourself to prepare possible answers for some or all the questions you have asked above and those written below. When you have finished your predictions, share your ideas with the class.

- Will Peter and Grandpa ever have any more wars while living in the same house?
- What professions will Peter, Billy, and Steve choose as adults?
- Will Jenny ever find out the details about the war between Peter and Grandpa?
- In the future, will the people in Peter's family discuss things before making decisions that involve family members?
- Does Grandpa ever meet someone and get married again?
- Does Grandpa ever move out?

Comments from the Class

Type in the following address for Amazon.com:

www.amazon.com

When arriving at this site, navigate to the book *The War with Grandpa*, and type in your comments about the story.

Grandparent Interview

Interview a grandparent about the important events in his or her life, including difficult and easy times. Share his or her comments with the class.

Game Board

Work in partners to create a game board on a 12" x 8" (30 cm x 20 cm) sheet of construction paper, based on what happens in the story. Think about the object of the game, how a player will move forward and backward, and what each space on the board will say.

Book Jacket

Create a book jacket for *The War with Grandpa*.

Venn Diagram

Make a Venn diagram, comparing and contrasting yourself with either Peter or Grandpa.

Final Storyboard

After reading *The War with Grandpa*, work in groups of two or three to complete a poster-size storyboard. Divide a large piece of tagboard into eight areas, similar to the diagram below.

1	2	3	4
5	6	7	8

1–Story Title

2–Main Characters

3–Setting of the Story

4–Problem or Conflict

5–Main Event

6–Main Event

7–Main Event

8–Solution/Ending

As a group, brainstorm and think of what to write and illustrate in each of the eight areas listed to the right of the diagram. Complete a rough draft of what your poster will look like when it is finished, and then work on the final draft. Share your group's poster with the class as your teacher prepares the following ocean treat.

Fish Delight

Ingredients

- three 6 oz. packages of lime gelatin

- 3–4 gummy fish per student

- whipped cream topping

Preparation

1. Prepare the lime gelatin according to the directions on the package.

2. Pour the gelatin into clear, small cups, filling each about half full.

3. Refrigerate the gelatin until it is slightly set and then add gummy fish to each cup.

4. When the gelatin is firm, top with the whipped topping and serve.

Letters from the Heart

After you finish reading *The War with Grandpa*, think about what Peter might say in a letter to Grandpa and what Grandpa might say in a letter to Peter after their war has ended. Use this page to write a letter to Grandpa from Peter, and then write a letter to Peter from Grandpa.

Dear Grandpa,

_____

_____

_____

_____

_____

_____

_____

_____

_____

Dear Peter,

_____

_____

_____

_____

_____

_____

_____

_____

_____

_____

Objective Test and Essay

Matching: Match the vocabulary word with the correct definition.

_____ 1. surrender

_____ 2. solemn

_____ 3. conceal

_____ 4. declaration

_____ 5. meander

_____ 6. dispute

_____ 7. tides

_____ 8. diabolical

_____ 9. revenge

_____ 10. fanatic

a. to make something known formally

b. an argument

c. someone who is excessively enthusiastic about something

d. alternate risings and fallings of the sea

e. inflict harm or injury for a wrong

f. very serious

g. hide

h. to give up oneself or a possession to another

i. wander aimlessly

j. fiendish

True or False: Write true or false next to each statement below.

_____ 1. Peter is writing this story because he is bored.

_____ 2. Grandpa Jack is moving in with Peter's family because he is lonely.

_____ 3. During Peter's first attack, he steals Grandpa's slippers.

_____ 4. Peter is a Risk fanatic.

_____ 5. Grandpa used to be in the construction business before he retired.

_____ 6. Because of Jenny, Peter gets his Monopoly pieces back from Grandpa.

_____ 7. After Peter moves back into his old room, his dad makes a sign for the door.

_____ 8. Grandpa's revenge involves a series of pranks played on Peter.

_____ 9. Peter is influenced by his friends to start the war with Grandpa.

_____ 10. According to Grandpa, fish like to feed when the tide is low.

Short Answers: Write a brief response to each question.

1. What is Peter's father's name, and what does he do for a living?

2. Why does Grandpa not say anything about the first note Peter writes to him?

3. What is the last thing Grandpa does for Peter in the story?

Essay: Respond to the following questions on a separate sheet of paper.

1. If you were Peter, what would you have done differently during the war, and what would you have done that was the same?

2. Would you like to have Peter's grandpa as your own grandpa? Why or why not? Give specific examples from the story that explain your reasoning.

3. What message do you think the author wanted to give any reader of this story?

Response

Explain the meanings of these quotations from *The War with Grandpa*. Support your ideas.

Chapter 2: *"I know something you don't," Jennifer said.*

Chapter 4: *"I love him up to the sky and down to the ocean."*

Chapter 7: *"Growing up, Pete," he said, "it isn't easy."*

Chapter 9: *"You're no Peapod anymore," he said.*

Chapter 9: *"There's no life in him," Mom said. "No life."*

Chapter 11: *"We'll have more fun than a barrel of monkeys."*

Chapter 12: *"Wishy-washy," Steve said. "What are you, a doormat?"*

Chapter 15: *"Isn't there something you read lately you want to talk about?" I asked.*

Chapter 18: *"Grandpa, I love you," I said, which made him smile. "But the war is still on!"*

Chapter 19: *"Soft hands are the secret."*

Chapter 20: *"You think you're one slippery customer, don't you?"*

Chapter 22: *"Pish-tosh."*

Chapter 22: *"Only a fool wants war."*

Chapter 24: *"My olfactory sense is working."*

Chapter 25: *"He has risen to the bait, don't you see?" said Steve.*

Chapter 26: *"Let's just say your Monopoly pieces are prisoners of war."*

Chapter 27: *"Ain't it great?" Grandpa grinned at me. "Just us two gents out on the road, footloose and fancy-free."*

Chapter 28: *"So," Grandpa said, "now we're playing hardball, eh?"*

Chapter 30: *"Who is The Old Man?" she asked.*

Chapter 34: *"All of us got off on the wrong foot."*

Conversations

Work in size-appropriate groups to write and perform the conversations that might have occurred in one of the following situations. If you prefer, you may use your own conversation idea for characters from *The War with Grandpa*.

- Grandpa, Mom, Dad, and Peter have a family conference to discuss what room Grandpa will stay in. (*4 people*)

- After Grandpa arrives at the Stokes', Peter tells him how he really feels about giving up his room. (*2 people*)

- Peter tells Billy and Steve about his first night in his new bedroom. (*3 people*)

- When Peter goes upstairs to say good night to Grandpa, Grandpa explains to Peter how special Grandma was to him and why he misses her so much. (*2 people*)

- Peter, Billy, and Steve collectively devise a plan to get Peter's room back. (*3 people*)

- Peter tells Jenny about the declaration of war that he wrote to Grandpa. (*2 people*)

- Instead of ignoring the declaration of war, Grandpa confronts Peter. (*2 people*)

- Peter describes his first attack strategy to Steve and Billy. (*3 people*)

- Grandpa decides to discuss the war with Peter and Mom at breakfast the morning after the first attack. (*3 people*)

- Steve explains to Peter and Billy why he likes school so much. (*3 people*)

- Instead of walking away from Grandpa after being slapped, Peter tries to talk things over with him. (*2 people*)

- Steve and Billy explain to Grandpa how Peter feels. (*3 people*)

- Instead of putting pressure on Peter to go to war with his Grandpa, Steve and Billy try to tell Peter that giving up his room is not a big deal. (*3 people*)

- Grandpa explains to Peter why he is fixing his rocker, even though they are in the middle of a war. (*2 people*)

- Peter and Grandpa discuss the war while they spend the day together fishing. (*2 people*)

- Grandpa catches Peter in the act of stealing his watch. (*2 people*)

- Grandpa tells Mom and Dad that he wants to switch rooms with Peter. (*3 people*)

- After school, Peter decides to tell his mom about Grandpa's revenge. (*2 people*)

- Peter and Grandpa explain to Jenny what is going on between them when she finds the note in the Monopoly game. (*3 people*)

- Peter tells Steve and Billy how the war ends. (*3 people*)

Bibliography of Related Reading

Fiction

Blume, Judy. *It's Not the End of the World*. Bradbury, 1972

    Then Again, Maybe I Won't. Dell, 1971

Byars, Betsy. *The Summer of the Swans*. Penguin, 1970

Carter, Forrest. *The Education of Little Tree*. Delacorte, 1976

Lowry, Lois. *All About Sam*. Yearling, 1989

    Number the Stars. Yearling, 1989

MacLachlan, Patricia. *Baby*. Dell, 1993

    Journey. Dell, 1991

    Through Grandpa's Eyes. HarperCollins, 1980

Smith, Robert Kimmel. *Bobby Baseball*. Yearling, 1991

    Chocolate Fever. Morrow, 1979

    Jelly Belly. Yearling, 1982

    Mostly Michael. Yearling, 1988

    The Squeaky Wheel. Dell, 1991

Nonfiction—Internet Curriculum Connections

American Civil War Home Page

    http://sunsite.utk.edu/civil-war/

Time Line of the Civil War, 1861–1865

    http://rs6.loc.gov/ammem/tl1861.html

Safari Touch Tank

    http://oberon.educ.sfu.ca/splash/tank.htm

The History Place: American Revolution

    http://www.historyplace.com/text-index.html

FINS: Everything you want to know about fish

    http://www.actwin.com/fish/index.html

Ocean Planet (Smithsonian)

    http://seawifs.gsfc.nasa.gov/ocean_planet.html

Sea World

    http://www.seaworld.org

Answer Key

Page 10
1. Responses will vary.
2. Responses will vary. Accept any logical reasoning.
3. Jennifer likes secrets.
4. Grandpa has been very lonely in Florida since Grandma died.
5. Responses will vary.
6. Jennifer still gets up during the night, and she still needs help getting dressed in the morning.
7. Peter probably likes to play games, color, and collect baseball cards.
8. The last thing to be moved into Peter's new room was Peter.
9. Responses will vary.
10. Peter is thinking about how he can get his room back.

Page 12
Accept correct answers for your state.

Page 14
1. He
2. She
3. It
4. She
5. It
6. They
7. We
8. he
9. I
10. He
11. He
12. They
13. It
14. They
15. I
16. he
17. We
18. you
19. They
20. We

Page 16
1. Responses will vary.
2. Peter's grandma died from emphysema.
3. They were always together.
4. Years ago a piece of wood fell on Grandpa's leg and broke it.
5. Grandpa's spirits are low, and he is grieving.
6. Grandpa rests when he mopes and stays in his room most of the time.
7. Responses will vary.
8. A fanatic is someone who is enthusiastic or very devoted to something. The rest of the answers will vary.
9. Responses will vary.
10. Peter starts the war by writing a declaration to Grandpa, but Grandpa ignores it.

Pages 18–19
Accept appropriate summaries.

Page 22
1. Responses will vary.
2. Billy and Steve do not think it is wise to start a war with a note.
3. During Peter's first attack, he sets Grandpa's alarm for 3:00 A.M.
4. Grandpa goes to Peter's room and is angry.
5. Responses will vary.
6. During Peter's second attack, he steals Grandpa's slippers.
7. Responses will vary.
8. Peter does not hide the slippers very well.
9. Peter cares deeply about his grandfather.
10. Responses will vary.

Page 23
Each star and stripe on the flag of the 13 Colonies stood for each colony at that time. Red, white, and blue were the king's colors.

Page 24
1. George Washington, Robert Morris, and George Ross visited Betsy Ross at her home and asked her to make the first flag for the United States.
2. Robert Peary cut the American flag into pieces and left them scattered at the North Pole.
3. Yes, but only in an emergency. It means, "Help me, I'm in trouble."
4. Flags are usually used until they are worn out and then they are destroyed, preferably by burning.
5. A vexillologist is an expert in the history of flags.
6. Francis Scott Key wrote "The Star-Spangled Banner" in 1814.
7. Alaska entered the Union in 1959, and Hawaii entered the Union in 1960.

Page 25
Accept all reasonable lists.

Page 26
1. disagreement, dispute
2. fumble, blunder
3. warrior, soldier
4. kin, family
5. prepare, fix
6. meander, roam
7. stubborn, bullheaded
8. surrender, give up
9. quit, retire
10. bother, annoy
11. chuckle, laugh
12. cease-fire, truce
13. capers, monkeyshines
14. elders, seniors
15. respect, admire
16. foe, enemy
17. devious, sneaky
18. plan, strategy
19. abnormal, unnatural
20. feud, fight

Page 28
1. Responses will vary.
2. Jenny does ballet routines during the lull.
3. Grandpa hides all the pieces to Peter's Monopoly game during his first counterattack.
4. Grandpa signs his note, "The Old Man."
5. Peter, Steve, and Billy get into an argument.
6. Responses will vary.
7. Grandpa is getting his sense of humor back.
8. Responses will vary.
9. Peter is going to steal Grandpa's wristwatch.
10. Jenny wants to play Monopoly so Steve returns the watch to Grandpa and in turn Grandpa returns the Monopoly game to Peter.

Page 30
1. There are 20,000 or more species of fish.
2. The whale shark is the world's largest fish.
3. The tiny goby is the world's smallest fish.
4. The bristlemouth is the most common fish in the sea.
5. Fish do not sleep in the same manner that humans do. They have no eyelids, but they rest by floating in place.
6. An anadromous fish spends most of its life in the sea, but it returns to fresh water to spawn.
7. A catadromous fish spends most of its life in fresh water, but it returns to the sea to spawn.
8. Age is determined by growth rings on scales and/or ringlike structures found in the small bones of the inner ear.
9. Fish live from a few weeks or months to 50 years or more.

Answer Key *(cont.)*

10. Fish who give birth to living young are called viviparous fish.
11. Fish breathe by absorbing oxygen from the water through their gills.
12. Fish usually swim 5–10 miles per hour. Tuna, however, can swim as fast as fifty miles per hour.
13. Members of the eel family can swim backwards.
14. Most fish swim in the horizontal position. A seahorse is an exception.
15. Fish do not chew their food because it would interfere with the passing of water over their gills.

Page 32

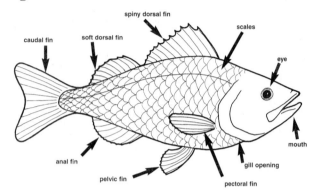

Page 34

1. Responses will vary.
2. Responses will vary.
3. Peter's radio alarm does not go off at the right time, his slippers are gone, his toothbrush is missing, his underwear is in the hall closet, his socks are in a cabinet in the bathroom, his flannel shirts and jeans have been turned inside out, the laces are missing from his sneakers, his books are missing, and he forgets his lunch.
4. Steve and Billy laugh like crazy.
5. Peter steals Grandpa's false teeth.
6. Responses will vary.
7. Responses will vary.
8. It helps Grandpa to get over his sadness.
9. Everyone should have had a family conference.
10. Grandpa fixes up the basement for himself, Dad's office is moved to the third floor, and Peter gets his room back.

Page 36
Accept any logical and reasonable diagrams.

Page 37
Across
4. OLDMAN
6. TEETH
9. ARTHUR
11. SIXTH
12. MOPE
15. MONOPOLY
16. FANATIC
17. RISK
18. FLORIDA
19. WARRIOR

Down
1. BALLET
2. JENNY
3. HIGHTIDE
5. FEUD
7. EMPHYSEMA
8. DIABOLICAL
9. ANNOY
10. TRUCE
13. CONSTRUCTION
14. RETALIATE

Page 38
Accept any logical and reasonable diagrams.

Page 39
Answers may vary.

Page 43
Matching
1. h	6. b
2. f	7. d
3. g	8. j
4. a	9. e
5. i	10. c

True or False
1. F
2. T
3. F
4. F
5. T
6. T
7. F
8. T
9. T
10. F

Short Answers
1. Arthur is an accountant.
2. Grandpa thought it was a joke.
3. Grandpa made a sign for Peter's door.